B·A·K·E
Your
D1122283

Dear Bakers,
We're looking forward to helping you bake your best. In preparation for this book, my staff in the Duncan Hines Kitchens have been busy developing, testing and tasting the recipes that follow. I've asked our home economists to come up with desserts and snacks that reflect the flavors of Fall and the approaching holiday season.

We've packed this book full of recipes you can use throughout this holiday season and beyond. There's special-occasion recipes, everyday recipes, no-cholesterol recipes and quick and easy recipes, plus many more for you to try. As an added touch, we've placed a special tip from our home economists at the end of each recipe. And all the recipes are written with clear step-by-step instructions, making it easier than ever for you to bake your best.

So browse through the pages that follow and enjoy all the wonderful recipes—we're sure you'll find the perfect dessert for almost any occasion.

Cindy Young
The Duncan Hines Kitchens

From left to right in the Duncan Hines Kitchens: Donna Lohr, Susan Waltman and Cindy Young

When you need recipe help, call our Duncan Hines Kitchen Connection. Whether you have questions about these recipes or about any of our fine products, help is just a toll-free phone call away. Let Duncan Hines help you bake your moist, delicious best. Our toll-free number is: 1-800-DH-MOIST. We hope to hear from you soon.

Gwen Hawk Brima
The Duncan Hines Kitchen Connection

From left to right our Kitchen Connection staff: Linda Holtgrafe, Wanda Kuyper, Barb Wilson, Carolyn Hibbard, Rosemarie O'Neill, Barb Fischer, Mary Grace Coddington, Gwen Hawk Brima and Anne Mae Scheper

HOLIDAY STRIPE CAKE

12 servings

1 package Duncan Hines® Moist Deluxe White Cake Mix
1 package (3 ounces) black cherry flavored gelatin
1 package (3 ounces) lime flavored gelatin
2 cups boiling water, divided
1 container (8 ounces) frozen whipped topping, thawed and divided
Red and green gum drops

1. Preheat oven to 350°F. Grease and flour two 8- or 9-inch round cake pans. Prepare, bake and cool cake following package directions.
2. Place cake layers top-sides up in two clean round cake pans. Punch holes in cake with fork in concentric circles.
3. Add 1 cup boiling water to each flavor gelatin in separate bowls; stir until dissolved. Pour black cherry gelatin slowly over first cake layer. Pour lime gelatin slowly over second cake layer. Refrigerate 3 hours or until gelatin is set.
4. Dip one cake pan in warm water 10 seconds. Invert cake layer onto serving plate. Spread 1 cup whipped topping on cake. Unmold second layer and carefully place on first layer. Frost top and sides with remaining whipped topping. Garnish with gum drops. Refrigerate until ready to serve.

Tip: Use your favorite flavor of red gelatin instead of black cherry.

Holiday Stripe Cake

RICH DOUBLE CHOCOLATE CREAM TORTE

8 to 12 servings

BROWNIE

1 package Duncan Hines® Brownies Plus Milk Chocolate Chunks Mix
3 eggs
⅓ cup water
⅓ cup Crisco® Oil or Puritan® Oil
½ cup finely chopped nuts

CHOCOLATE BUTTER CREAM

1 package (6 ounces) semi-sweet chocolate chips, melted
½ cup butter or margarine, softened
1 cup whipping cream, chilled and divided

WHIPPED CREAM

2 tablespoons sugar
1 tablespoon chocolate jimmies

1. Preheat oven to 350°F. Grease and flour 9-inch round pan.
2. **For brownie,** combine brownie mix, eggs, water, oil and nuts. Stir with spoon until well blended, about 50 strokes. Pour into pan. Bake at 350°F for 35 to 40 minutes. Cool 30 minutes. Run knife around edge of pan. Invert onto serving platter.
3. **For chocolate butter cream,** stir together melted chocolate, butter and 2 tablespoons whipping cream. Spread over top of brownie.
4. **For whipped cream,** beat remaining whipping cream and sugar with electric mixer on high speed for 1 to 3 minutes or until thick. Spread over chocolate butter cream. Sprinkle with chocolate jimmies. Refrigerate until ready to serve.

Tip: Chilling the beaters and bowl before whipping the cream decreases whipping time and helps insure good volume.

CHERRY CHOCOLATE CHIP COOKIES

3½ to 4 dozen

1 package Duncan Hines® Moist Deluxe Yellow Cake Mix
½ cup butter or margarine, melted
1 egg
1 package (6 ounces) semi-sweet chocolate chips
½ cup chopped pecans
¼ cup chopped maraschino cherries, drained

1. Preheat oven to 375°F.
2. Combine cake mix, butter and egg in large bowl. Stir in chocolate chips, pecans and maraschino cherries.
3. Drop by slightly rounded teaspoonfuls onto ungreased baking sheets. Bake at 375°F for 10 to 12 minutes or until lightly browned. Cool 1 minute on baking sheet. Remove to cooling rack.

Tip: For a festive holiday appearance, use both red *and* green maraschino cherries.

Rich Double Chocolate Cream Torte

BROWNIE ALASKA

2 brownie alaskas, 8 to 10 servings, each

1 package Duncan Hines® Brownies Plus Double Fudge Mix
½ gallon brick strawberry ice cream
6 egg whites
2 cups marshmallow creme

1. Preheat oven to 350°F. Line 13 × 9 × 2-inch pan with aluminum foil.
2. Prepare, bake and cool brownie mix following package directions.
3. Invert brownie onto cookie sheet. Remove foil and cut in half crosswise so each half measures 8½ × 6½-inches. Cut brick ice cream in half lengthwise. Place each half on brownie halves. Chill in freezer.
4. For meringue, preheat oven to 475°F. Beat egg whites until soft peaks form. Add marshmallow creme, ¼ cup at a time. Beat well after each addition. Beat until stiff peaks form. Divide between two brownie halves. Spread over top and sides sealing edges completely. Bake at 475°F for 2 to 3 minutes or until meringue has browned. Serve immediately.

Note: Recipe makes two Brownie Alaskas; one to serve and one to freeze for a quick dessert at a later time. To freeze, loosely wrap with aluminum foil.

Tip: For delicious variations, try different ice creams such as mint chocolate chip, peppermint or chocolate.

Brownie Alaska

FUDGE RUM BALLS

6 dozen

- 1 package Duncan Hines® Moist Deluxe Butter Recipe Fudge Cake Mix
- 1 cup finely chopped pecans or walnuts
- 1 tablespoon rum extract
- 2 cups sifted confectioners sugar
- ¼ cup unsweetened cocoa
- Pecans or walnuts, finely chopped

1. Preheat oven to 375°F. Grease and flour 13 × 9 × 2-inch pan. Prepare, bake and cool cake following package directions.
2. Crumble cake into large bowl. Stir with fork until crumbs are fine and uniform in size. Add 1 cup nuts, rum extract, confectioners sugar and cocoa. Stir until well blended.
3. Shape heaping tablespoonfuls mixture into balls. Garnish by rolling balls in finely chopped nuts. Press firmly to adhere nuts to balls.

Tip: Substitute real rum for rum extract.

GRASSHOPPER DESSERT

12 servings

CRUST
- 1 package Duncan Hines® Moist Deluxe Dark Dutch Fudge Cake Mix, divided
- 1 egg
- ½ cup butter or margarine, softened

FILLING
- 3 cups miniature marshmallows
- ½ cup milk
- ⅓ cup green creme de menthe
- 2 tablespoons white creme de cacao
- 1½ cups whipping cream

1. Preheat oven to 350°F. Grease and flour 13 × 9 × 2-inch pan. Remove ½ cup cake mix and spread in 8-inch ungreased baking pan. Toast in oven for 7 minutes. Cool.
2. **For crust**, combine remaining cake mix, egg and butter in large bowl. Mix until crumbs form. Press lightly into prepared 13 × 9 × 2-inch pan. Bake at 350°F for 15 minutes. Cool.
3. **For filling**, heat marshmallows and milk in medium saucepan over low heat. Stir constantly until marshmallows melt. Refrigerate until thickened. Stir creme de menthe and creme de cacao into marshmallow mixture.
4. Beat whipping cream until stiff in large bowl. Fold in marshmallow mixture. Pour into crust. Dust top with toasted dry mix. Refrigerate until ready to serve. Cut into 3-inch squares.

Tip: To quickly chill marshmallow mixture, pour mixture into medium bowl, place in larger bowl of ice water and refrigerate; stir occasionally.

Fudge Rum Balls

BANANA CREAM CHEESECAKE

12 servings

1 package Duncan Hines® Moist Deluxe Banana Supreme Cake Mix
1 can (8 ounces) crushed pineapple, drained and juice reserved
1 package (4-serving size) vanilla instant pudding and pie filling mix
4 eggs
½ cup Crisco® Oil or Puritan® Oil
½ teaspoon ground cinnamon
½ cup sliced banana
½ cup finely chopped pecans or walnuts
¼ cup chopped maraschino cherries, drained
1 container (16 ounces) Duncan Hines® Cream Cheese Frosting

1. Preheat oven to 350°F. Grease and flour two 9-inch round cake pans.
2. **For cake**, add water to reserved pineapple juice to equal 1 cup. Combine cake mix, pudding mix, pineapple and the 1 cup pineapple liquid, eggs, oil and cinnamon in large bowl. Beat at medium speed with electric mixer for 2 minutes. Stir in banana slices, nuts and cherries. Pour into pans. Bake at 350°F for 40 to 45 minutes or until toothpick inserted in center comes out clean. Cool in pans 15 minutes. Invert onto cooling racks. Cool completely.
3. Fill and frost with cream cheese frosting.

Tip: Garnish top of cake with additional nuts, if desired.

CHOCOLATE LACE VALENTINE CAKE

16 to 20 servings

1 package Duncan Hines® Moist Deluxe Devil's Food Cake Mix
1 container (16 ounces) Duncan Hines® Frosting (any flavor)
3 bars (1.55 ounces each) milk chocolate, melted

1. Preheat oven to 350°F. Grease and flour 13 × 9 × 2-inch pan. Prepare, bake and cool cake following package directions.
2. Frost top of cake with chocolate frosting. Draw heart outline in frosting with tip of knife. Place melted chocolate in decorating bag with small writing tip. Outline heart shape with chocolate. Write "Be Mine" in center of heart. Drizzle remaining chocolate in bag around outside of heart to form lace.

Tip: If a decorating tip and bag are not available, try using a small plastic bag. Fill with chocolate and snip off a tiny corner to use as a tip.

HEART AND KISSES CAKE

16 to 20 servings

1 package Duncan Hines® Moist Deluxe Cake Mix (any flavor)
5 cups confectioners sugar
¾ cup Crisco® Shortening
½ cup water
⅓ cup non-dairy creamer
2 teaspoons vanilla extract
½ teaspoon salt
Red food coloring
Chocolate kiss candies

1. Preheat oven to 350°F. Grease and flour one 8-inch round and one 8-inch square pan.
2. For cake, prepare cake as directed on package. Pour 2 cups batter into round pan and 3 cups batter into square pan. Bake and cool cake following package directions.
3. For frosting, combine confectioners sugar, shortening, water, non-dairy creamer, vanilla extract and salt in large bowl. Beat at medium speed with electric mixer for 3 minutes. Beat at high speed for 5 minutes. Add more confectioners sugar to thicken or more water to thin as needed. Reserve 1½ cups frosting for decorating, if desired. Tint remaining frosting pink with red food coloring.
4. Place square cake on serving platter bottom side up. Cut round cake in half. Place each half top side up next to square as shown in diagram. Spread pink frosting on cake. Use reserved frosting for writing Valentine greeting and decorating edges. Garnish with chocolate kiss candies.

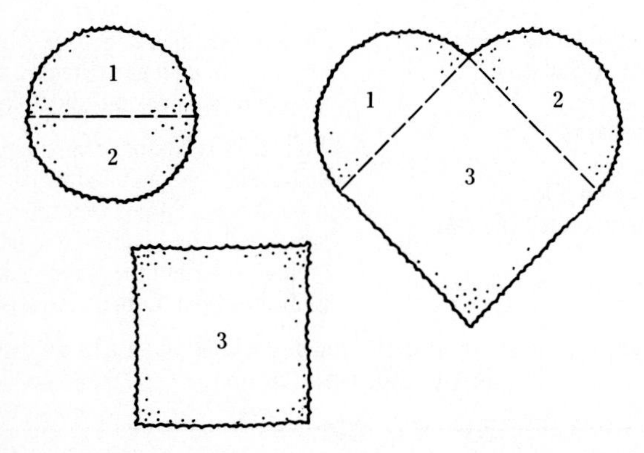

Tip: For a lovely presentation, assemble cake on large cookie sheet or serving platter covered with lace doilies.

STRAWBERRY ICE CREAM CAKE

12 to 16 servings

1 package Duncan Hines® Moist Deluxe Strawberry Supreme Cake Mix

RUM SYRUP
⅓ cup boiling water
⅓ cup sugar
⅓ cup cold water
¼ cup dark rum

FILLING AND FROSTING
1 pint strawberry ice cream, softened
1 container (8 ounces) frozen whipped topping, thawed
Fresh strawberries, for garnish

1. Preheat oven to 350°F. Grease and flour two 9-inch round cake pans. Prepare, bake and cool cake following package directions.

2. **For rum syrup,** stir boiling water into sugar in medium bowl. Stir until sugar is dissolved. Add cold water and rum. Cool.

3. Place cake layers on cooling racks on jelly roll pan. Spoon ½ cup rum syrup evenly over each layer. Freeze 2 hours or until firm.

4. Place one cake layer on serving plate. Spread softened ice cream to edges. Place second layer on top of ice cream. Freeze assembled cake until ice cream is firm.

5. Frost sides and top with whipped topping. Garnish with fresh strawberries, if desired. Store in freezer until ready to serve.

Tip: Allow cake to stand at room temperature 10 to 15 minutes before serving. For easiest cutting, use a knife with a thin sharp blade.

BROILED ORANGE APRICOT CAKE

12 to 16 servings

1 package Duncan Hines® Moist Deluxe Orange Supreme Cake Mix
1 jar (12 ounces) apricot preserves
1 tablespoon lemon juice
1 can (3½ ounces) flaked coconut (1⅓ cups)
2 cups miniature marshmallows

1. Preheat oven to 350°F. Grease and flour 13 × 9 × 2-inch pan. Prepare and bake cake following package directions.

2. While cake is baking, combine preserves, lemon juice, coconut and marshmallows in small bowl. Spread over top of hot cake. Broil 3 or 4 inches from heat about 2 minutes or until the marshmallows are lightly browned. Cool before serving.

Tip: To prevent marshmallows from sticking to the knife you use to cut the cake, wet the blade before cutting.

Strawberry Ice Cream Cake

CHOCOLATE DREAM TORTE

12 servings

1 package Duncan Hines® Moist Deluxe Dark Dutch Fudge Cake Mix
1 package (6 ounces) semi-sweet chocolate chips, melted, for garnish
1 container (8 ounces) frozen whipped topping, thawed and divided
1 container (16 ounces) Duncan Hines® Milk Chocolate Frosting
3 tablespoons finely chopped dry roasted pistachios

1. Preheat oven to 350°F. Grease and flour two 9-inch round cake pans. Prepare, bake and cool cake following package directions.

2. **For chocolate hearts garnish,** spread melted chocolate to ⅛-inch thickness on waxed-paper-lined cookie sheet. Cut shapes with heart cookie cutter when chocolate begins to set. Refrigerate until firm. Push out heart shapes. Set aside.

3. Split each cake layer in half horizontally. Spread one-third whipped topping on one cake layer. Place second layer on top of filling. Repeat with remaining layers. Frost sides and top with milk chocolate frosting. Sprinkle pistachios on top. Position chocolate hearts by pushing points down into cake. Refrigerate until ready to serve.

Tip: Melt chocolate chips in the top of a double boiler over hot, not boiling, water. Stir until smooth. Or melt chips in microwave oven: place in microwave-safe bowl and microwave at MEDIUM (50% power) 1 to 1½ minutes; stir until smooth.

CHERRY PINEAPPLE TRIFLE

24 large or 32 small servings

1 package Duncan Hines® Moist Deluxe Yellow Cake Mix
1 package (4-serving size) vanilla instant pudding and pie filling mix
1 can (15¼ ounces) crushed pineapple, drained
1 can (21 ounces) cherry pie filling
1 package (12 ounces) flaked coconut (3½ cups)
2 cups chopped pecans
2 containers (8 ounces each) frozen whipped topping, thawed

1. Preheat oven to 350°F. Grease and flour two 9-inch round cake pans. Prepare, bake and cool cake following package directions.

2. Prepare instant pudding following directions. Refrigerate until ready to use.

3. Crumble one cake layer in 6-quart trifle dish. Layer half each of pudding, pineapple, cherry pie filling, coconut, pecans and whipped topping. Repeat layers, beginning with crumbling second cake layer. Top with remaining pecans. Refrigerate until ready to serve.

Tip: If a trifle dish is not available, use a 6-quart clear glass bowl with straight sides.

Chocolate Dream Torte

CHRISTMAS TREE CAKE

16 to 20 servings

1 package Duncan Hines® Moist Deluxe Cake Mix (any flavor)
5 cups confectioners sugar
¾ cup Crisco® Shortening
½ cup water
⅓ cup non-dairy creamer
2 teaspoons vanilla extract
½ teaspoon salt
1 tablespoon green food coloring
Peppermint candies
Pretzel rods
Large gumdrops

1. Preheat oven to 350°F. Grease and flour 13 × 9 × 2-inch pan. Prepare, bake and cool cake following package directions.

2. **For decorator frosting,** combine confectioners sugar, shortening, water, non-dairy creamer, vanilla extract and salt in large bowl. Beat at medium speed with electric mixer for 3 minutes. Beat at high speed for 5 minutes. Add more confectioners sugar to thicken or more water to thin as needed. Reserve 1 cup frosting. Tint remaining frosting with green food coloring.

3. Cut cooled cake and arrange as shown. Spread green frosting over cake. Decorate tree with reserved white frosting and peppermint candies. Make tree trunk of pretzel rods. Roll out large gumdrop and cut with star cookie cutter. Top tree with gumdrop star.

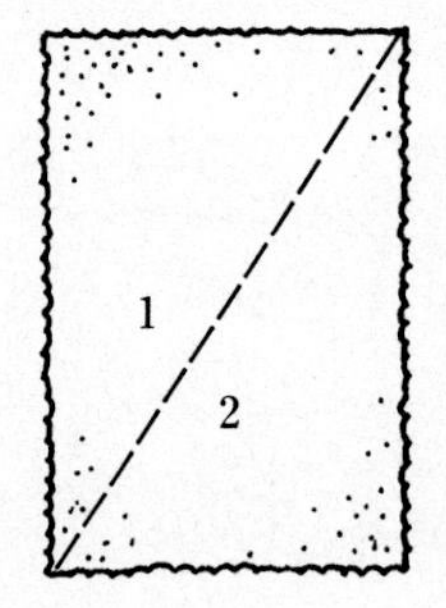

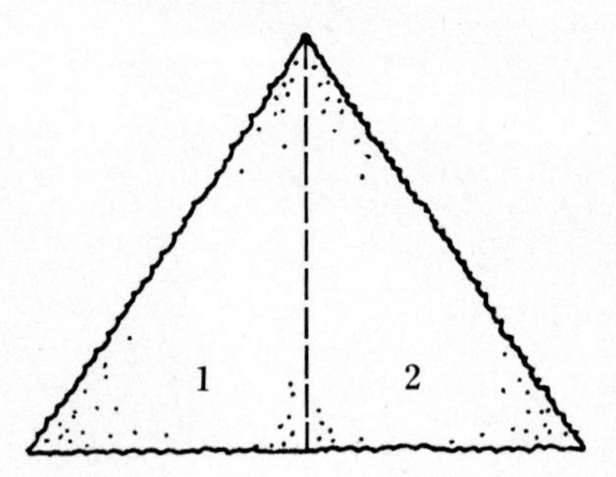

Tip: To make the garland, pipe frosting using a pastry bag fitted with a star tip, or use red rope licorice.

Christmas Tree Cake

PINK PEPPERMINT SURPRISE

12 to 16 servings

1 package Duncan Hines® Angel Food Cake Mix
1 teaspoon peppermint extract
6 to 8 drops red food coloring
½ gallon vanilla ice cream
½ cup chocolate fudge ice cream topping
Peppermint candies, crushed

1. Preheat oven to 375°F.
2. For cake, add peppermint extract and 6 to 8 drops food coloring to egg white packet and water. Prepare, bake and cool cake following package directions.
3. Serve each cake slice with vanilla ice cream, chocolate fudge ice cream topping and crushed peppermint candy.

Tip: To slice cake, use a serrated knife and cut in a sawing motion.

CREAMY EGGNOG DESSERT

12 to 16 servings

CRUST
1 package Duncan Hines® Moist Deluxe Swiss Chocolate Cake Mix
½ cup butter or margarine, melted
½ cup chopped pecans

FILLING
1 package (8 ounces) cream cheese, softened
1 cup sugar
1 container (12 ounces) frozen whipped topping, thawed and divided
2 packages (4-serving size each) french vanilla instant pudding and pie filling mix
3 cups cold milk
¼ teaspoon rum extract
¼ teaspoon ground nutmeg

1. Preheat oven to 350°F.
2. **For crust**, combine cake mix, butter and pecans. Reserve ½ cup mixture. Press remaining mixture into bottom of 13 × 9 × 2-inch pan. Bake at 350°F for 15 to 20 minutes or until surface is firm. Cool. Toast reserved ½ cup mixture on cookie sheet at 350°F for 3 to 4 minutes, stirring once. Cool completely. Break lumps with fork to make small crumbs.
3. **For filling,** beat cream cheese and sugar until smooth in large bowl. Stir in 1 cup whipped topping. Spread over cooled crust. Refrigerate. Combine pudding mix and milk; beat 1 minute. Add rum extract and nutmeg. Spread over cheese layer. Spread remaining whipped topping over pudding layer. Sprinkle with reserved toasted mixture. Refrigerate at least 2 hours.

Tip: For best results, be sure to use standard measuring spoons and cups that are in good condition.

Pink Peppermint Surprise

FUDGE MARBLE PISTACHIO CAKE

12 to 16 servings

CAKE
- 1 package Duncan Hines® Moist Deluxe Fudge Marble Cake Mix
- 1 package (4-serving size) pistachio instant pudding and pie filling mix
- 4 eggs
- 1 cup water
- ⅓ cup Crisco® Oil or Puritan® Oil
- 5 or 6 drops green food coloring

FROSTING
- 1 package (4-serving size) pistachio instant pudding and pie filling mix
- 2 envelopes whipped topping mix
- 1¼ cups cold milk
- Green food coloring (optional)
- Chocolate curls or grated chocolate

1. Preheat oven to 350°F. Grease and flour 10-inch tube pan or Bundt® pan.
2. **For cake,** set aside cocoa packet. Combine cake mix, pudding mix, eggs, water, oil and food coloring in large bowl. Beat at medium speed with electric mixer for 2 minutes. Measure 1 cup batter. Place in small bowl. Stir in cocoa packet. Spoon half of green batter into pan. Drizzle half of chocolate batter over top. Repeat. Run knife through batters to marble. Bake at 350°F for 50 to 60 minutes or until toothpick inserted in center comes out clean. Cool in pan 25 minutes. Invert cake onto serving plate. Cool completely.
3. **For frosting,** combine pudding mix, whipped topping mix and milk in large bowl. Beat 2 to 3 minutes or until stiff. Beat in green food coloring, if desired. Frost cooled cake. Decorate with chocolate curls or grated chocolate.

Tip: To make chocolate curls, use sharp vegetable peeler to slice across block of milk chocolate. Use long, thin strokes. Slide toothpick into curl to transfer to cake.

CHOCOLATE RASPBERRY CAKE

12 to 16 servings

- 1 package Duncan Hines® Moist Deluxe Devil's Food Cake Mix
- ½ cup seedless raspberry jam
- 3 cups frozen whipped topping, thawed

1. Preheat oven to 350°F. Grease and flour two 9-inch round cake pans. Prepare, bake and cool cake following package directions.
2. To assemble, place one cake layer on serving plate. Spread thin layer of jam over cake. Place second layer on top.
3. Stir remaining jam until smooth. Fold into whipped topping. Frost cake with topping mixture. Garnish with additional whipped topping and jam, if desired.

Tip: You may use other flavor preserves or jams in place of raspberry jam.

Fudge Marble Pistachio Cake

PARTY SQUARES

16 servings

1 package Duncan Hines® Moist Deluxe Swiss Chocolate Cake Mix
1 container (12 ounces) Duncan Hines® Vanilla Sheetcake Frosting, divided
Red food coloring
2 bars (1.55 ounces each) milk chocolate

1. Preheat oven to 350°F. Grease and flour 13 × 9 × 2-inch pan. Prepare, bake and cool cake following package directions.
2. Reserve ⅓ cup of the frosting. Tint remaining frosting pink with red food coloring. Frost cake with pink frosting. Using a spatula, make diagonal lines in frosting across top of cake. Mark 16 servings with tip of knife.
3. Cut milk chocolate bars into sections according to division marks on bars. Place chocolate pieces on top of each serving. Place star tip in pastry bag; fill with reserved frosting. Pipe star partially on each chocolate piece to anchor. Cut cake into servings following lines in frosting.

Tip: This simple cake has many decorating options. Try reserving ⅓ cup frosting and tinting with green food coloring. Leave remaining frosting white. Decorate as above except fit pastry bag with leaf tip.

Party Squares

JAMAICAN BANANA CAKE

16 to 20 servings

CAKE
1 package Duncan Hines® Moist Deluxe Banana Supreme Cake Mix
½ cup finely chopped walnuts

BROILED TOPPING
¾ cup firmly packed brown sugar
⅓ cup Butter Flavor Crisco®
2 tablespoons milk
1 cup flaked coconut
⅓ cup chopped walnuts

1. Preheat oven to 350°F. Grease and flour 13 × 9 × 2-inch pan.
2. Prepare cake mix as directed on package. Stir in ½ cup finely chopped walnuts. Pour into pan. Bake at 350°F for 33 to 38 minutes or until toothpick inserted in center comes out clean.
3. **For topping,** set oven to broil. Combine brown sugar, Butter Flavor Crisco® and milk in small saucepan. Cook over medium heat, stirring constantly for 2 minutes, or until shortening melts. Stir in coconut and ⅓ cup walnuts. Spread over warm cake. Broil 4 inches from heat 2 to 3 minutes or until golden. Cool completely.

Tip: Rotate cake under broiler for more even browning.

PECAN DIPPED CHOCOLATE CAKE

16 to 20 servings

1 package Duncan Hines® Moist Deluxe Devil's Food Cake Mix
1 container (12 ounces) Duncan Hines® Chocolate Sheetcake Frosting, divided
25 to 30 pecan halves

1. Preheat oven to 350°F. Grease and flour 13 × 9 × 2-inch pan. Prepare, bake and cool cake following package directions.
2. Measure ¼ cup chocolate frosting into small microwave-safe measuring cup. Microwave at HIGH (100% power) for 15 seconds; stir until smooth. Dip bottom third of pecan halves in melted frosting. Place on waxed-paper-lined baking sheet. Refrigerate 10 minutes or until set. Stir melted frosting into remaining frosting in container.
3. Frost cake with chocolate frosting. Arrange dipped pecans as desired to decorate cake.

Tip: For uniformity choose pecan halves that are all approximately the same size.

Jamaican Banana Cake

CAPPUCINO BON BONS

40 bon bons

1 package Duncan Hines® Fudge Brownie Mix, Family Size
2 eggs
⅓ cup water
⅓ cup Crisco® Oil or Puritan® Oil
1½ tablespoons Folgers® Instant Coffee
1 teaspoon ground cinnamon
Whipped topping
Cinnamon

1. Preheat oven to 350°F. Place 2-inch foil cupcake liners on cookie sheet.
2. Combine brownie mix, eggs, water, oil, instant coffee and cinnamon. Stir with spoon until well blended, about 50 strokes. Fill each cupcake liner with 1 measuring tablespoon batter. Bake at 350°F for 12 to 15 minutes or until toothpick inserted in center comes out clean. Cool completely. Garnish with whipped topping and a dash of cinnamon. Refrigerate until ready to serve.

Tip: To make larger Bon Bons, use twelve 2½-inch foil cupcake liners and fill with ¼ cup batter. Bake for 28 to 30 minutes.

GOLDEN OATMEAL MUFFINS

2 dozen

1 package Duncan Hines® Moist Deluxe Butter Recipe Golden Cake Mix
1 cup quick-cooking oats
¼ teaspoon salt
¾ cup milk
2 eggs, slightly beaten
2 tablespoons butter or margarine, melted

1. Preheat oven to 400°F. Grease 24 (2½ inch) muffin cups (or use paper liners).
2. Combine cake mix, oats and salt in large bowl. Add milk, eggs and melted butter; stir until moistened. Fill muffin cups two-thirds full. Bake at 400°F for 13 minutes or until golden brown. Serve with honey or your favorite jam.

Tip: For a slightly different flavor, try adding 1 teaspoon ground cinnamon with the dry ingredients.

Cappucino Bon Bons

PECAN DATE BARS

32 bars

CRUST
- 1 package Duncan Hines® Moist Deluxe White Cake Mix
- ⅓ cup butter or margarine
- 1 egg

TOPPING
- 1 package (8 ounces) chopped dates
- 1¼ cups chopped pecans
- 1 cup water
- ½ teaspoon vanilla extract
- Confectioners sugar

1. Preheat oven to 350°F. Grease and flour 13 × 9 × 2-inch pan.
2. **For crust**, cut butter into cake mix with a pastry blender or 2 knives until mixture is crumbly. Add egg; stir well (mixture will be crumbly). Pat mixture into bottom of pan.
3. **For topping**, combine dates, pecans and water in medium saucepan. Bring to a boil. Reduce heat and simmer until mixture thickens, stirring constantly. Remove from heat. Stir in vanilla extract. Spread date mixture evenly over crust. Bake at 350°F for 25 to 30 minutes. Cool completely. Dust with confectioners sugar.

Tip: Pecan Date Bars are moist and store well in airtight containers. Dust with confectioners sugar to freshen before serving.

TAKE-ALONG CAKE

12 to 16 servings

- 1 package Duncan Hines® Moist Deluxe Swiss Chocolate Cake Mix
- 1 package (12 ounces) semi-sweet chocolate chips
- 1 cup miniature marshmallows
- ¼ cup butter or margarine, melted
- ½ cup firmly packed brown sugar
- ½ cup chopped pecans or walnuts

1. Preheat oven to 350°F. Grease and flour 13 × 9 × 2-inch pan.
2. Prepare cake following package directions. Add chocolate chips and marshmallows to batter. Pour into pan. Drizzle melted butter over batter. Sprinkle with brown sugar and top with nuts. Bake at 350°F for 45 to 55 minutes.

Tip: Chocolate should be stored in a cool, dry place. When the storage area becomes too warm, chocolate will develop "bloom" or a visible gray coating. Bloom has no effect on either the flavor or the quality of the chocolate and you may still use the chocolate in baking with excellent results.

Pecan Date Bars

PECAN FUDGE SHEETCAKE

20 servings

1 package Duncan Hines® Moist Deluxe Devil's Food Cake Mix
½ cup butter or margarine
¼ cup plus 2 tablespoons milk
¼ cup unsweetened cocoa
1 pound confectioners sugar (3½ to 4 cups)
1 teaspoon vanilla extract
¾ cup chopped pecans

1. Preheat oven to 350°F. Grease 15½ × 10½ × 1-inch pan. Prepare cake following package directions. Pour batter into pan. Bake at 350°F for 20 to 25 minutes or until toothpick inserted in center comes out clean.
2. For frosting, combine butter, milk and cocoa in medium saucepan. Stir over low heat until butter is melted. Add confectioners sugar and vanilla extract, stirring until smooth. Stir in pecans. Pour over warm cake. Cool completely.

Tip: For best results, allow the cake to cool undisturbed until frosting is set, about 4 hours.

PEANUTTY ORANGE CAKE

16 to 20 servings

1 package Duncan Hines® Moist Deluxe Orange Supreme Cake Mix
¾ cup firmly packed brown sugar
¼ cup butter or margarine
⅔ cup Jif® Creamy Peanut Butter
¼ cup milk
¾ cup chopped peanuts

1. Preheat oven to 350°F. Grease and flour 13 × 9 × 2-inch pan. Prepare and bake cake following package directions.
2. For topping, combine brown sugar, butter, peanut butter and milk in medium saucepan. Stir over medium heat until warm and smooth. Remove from heat. Stir in peanuts. Spread topping over warm cake. Broil 3 inches from heat 1 minute or until golden brown. Cool.

Tip: Also delicious using Duncan Hines® Moist Deluxe Banana Supreme Cake Mix.

Pecan Fudge Sheet Cake

APRICOT PECAN LOAF

12 slices

1 package Duncan Hines® Bakery Style Pecan Crunch with Crumb Topping Muffin Mix
1 egg
⅔ cup water
¼ cup apricot preserves

1. Preheat oven to 350°F. Grease one 8 × 4-inch or 9 × 5-inch loaf pan.
2. Combine muffin mix and topping mix in large bowl. Blend in egg and water. Pour batter into pan. Drop preserves onto batter by teaspoonfuls. Swirl into batter with knife. Bake at 350°F for 45 to 55 minutes or until toothpick inserted in center comes out clean. Cool in pan 10 minutes. Loosen loaf from pan. Invert onto cooling rack. Turn right side up. Cool completely. Dust with confectioners sugar, if desired.

Tip: When you test doneness by inserting a toothpick in the center of the loaf, it should come out dry and free of crumbs.

CHOCOLATE TOFFEE PECAN CAKE

8 to 10 servings

CAKE
1 package Duncan Hines® Moist Deluxe Devil's Food Cake Mix
1 package (4-serving size) chocolate instant pudding and pie filling mix
4 eggs
1¼ cups water
½ cup Crisco® Oil or Puritan® Oil
1½ cups chopped pecans, divided
1 cup butterscotch flavored chips
½ cup almond brickle chips

GLAZE
1 package (12 ounces) sweet or semi-sweet chocolate chips
¼ cup plus 2 tablespoons butter or margarine

1. Preheat oven to 350°F. Grease and flour 10-inch Bundt® pan.
2. **For cake,** combine cake mix, pudding mix, eggs, water, oil, 1 cup pecans, butterscotch and brickle chips in large bowl. Beat at medium speed with electric mixer for 2 minutes. Pour into pan. Bake at 350°F for 55 to 60 minutes or until toothpick inserted in center comes out clean. Cool in pan 25 minutes. Invert onto serving plate.
3. **For glaze,** combine chocolate chips and butter in small saucepan. Heat over low heat until chips are melted; stir until smooth (glaze will be very thick). Spoon hot glaze over cooled cake. Garnish with remaining ½ cup pecans.

Tip: You can prepare the glaze in the microwave oven. Place chips and butter in microwave-safe bowl and microwave at MEDIUM (50% power) for 1½ minutes; stir. Microwave at MEDIUM an additional 1½ minutes, or until chips are melted and smooth when stirred.

PINEAPPLE ORANGE TORTE

12 servings

CAKE
- 1 package Duncan Hines® Moist Deluxe Pineapple Supreme Cake Mix
- 4 eggs
- ½ cup butter or margarine, softened
- ¼ cup Crisco® Oil or Puritan® Oil
- 1 can (11 ounces) mandarin oranges with juice

FILLING AND TOPPING
- 1 can (20 ounces) crushed pineapple with juice
- 1 package (4-serving size) vanilla instant pudding and pie filling mix
- 1 container (8 ounces) frozen whipped topping, thawed

1. Preheat oven to 350°F. Grease and flour three 9-inch round cake pans.
2. **For cake,** combine cake mix, eggs, butter and oil in large bowl. Add oranges with juice. Beat at medium speed with electric mixer until blended. Pour into pans. Bake at 350°F for 30 to 35 minutes or until toothpick inserted in center comes out clean. Cool in pans 15 minutes. Invert onto cooling rack. Cool completely.
3. **For filling and topping,** combine pineapple with juice and pudding mix in medium bowl. Beat at medium speed with electric mixer for 2 minutes. Fold in whipped topping. Refrigerate 15 to 20 minutes.
4. To assemble, spread filling between cake layers; frost top only with remaining filling. Refrigerate until ready to serve.

Tip: If desired, reserve several orange sections and 1 tablespoon pineapple for garnish.

DOUBLE CHOCOLATE CREAM CAKE

16 to 20 servings

- 1 package Duncan Hines® Moist Deluxe Butter Recipe Fudge Cake Mix
- 1 envelope whipped topping mix
- ½ cup chocolate syrup
- Maraschino cherries with stems, for garnish

1. Preheat oven to 375°F. Grease and flour 13 × 9 × 2-inch pan. Prepare, bake and cool cake following package directions.
2. For topping, prepare whipped topping mix following package directions. Fold in chocolate syrup until blended. Refrigerate until ready to serve.
3. Spoon chocolate cream topping over cake slices to serve. Garnish with maraschino cherries.

Tip: For best consistency, chill chocolate syrup before using.

PINEAPPLE UPSIDE DOWN CAKE

16 to 20 servings

TOPPING
- ½ cup butter or margarine
- 1 cup firmly packed brown sugar
- 1 can (20 ounces) pineapple slices, well drained
- Maraschino cherries, halved and drained
- Walnut halves

CAKE
- 1 package Duncan Hines® Moist Deluxe Pineapple Supreme Cake Mix
- 1 package (4-serving size) vanilla instant pudding and pie filling mix
- 4 eggs
- 1 cup water
- ½ cup Crisco® Oil or Puritan® Oil

1. Preheat oven to 350°F.
2. **For topping,** melt butter over low heat in 12-inch cast-iron skillet or skillet with oven-proof handle. Remove from heat. Stir in brown sugar. Spread to cover bottom of skillet. Arrange pineapple slices, maraschino cherries and walnut halves in skillet. Set aside.
3. **For cake,** combine cake mix, pudding mix, eggs, water and oil in large mixing bowl. Beat at medium speed with electric mixer for 2 minutes. Pour batter evenly over fruit in skillet. Bake at 350°F for 1 hour or until toothpick inserted in center comes out clean. Invert onto serving plate.

Tip: Cake can be made in a 13 × 9 × 2-inch pan. Bake at 350°F for 45 to 55 minutes or until toothpick inserted in center comes out clean. Cake is also delicious using Duncan Hines® Moist Deluxe Yellow Cake Mix.

Pineapple Upside Down Cake

TOFFEE BROWNIE BARS

48 bars

CRUST
- ¾ cup butter or margarine, softened
- ¾ cup firmly packed brown sugar
- 1 egg yolk
- ¾ teaspoon vanilla extract
- 1½ cups all-purpose flour

FILLING
- 1 package Duncan Hines® Fudge Brownie Mix, Family Size
- 1 egg
- ⅓ cup water
- ⅓ cup Crisco® Oil or Puritan® Oil

TOPPING
- 1 package (12 ounces) milk chocolate chips, melted
- ¾ cup finely chopped pecans

1. Preheat oven to 350°F. Grease 15½ × 10½ × 1 inch pan.
2. **For crust**, combine butter, brown sugar, egg yolk and vanilla extract in large bowl. Stir in flour. Spread in pan. Bake 15 minutes or until golden.
3. **For filling**, prepare brownie mix following package directions. Spread over hot crust. Bake 15 minutes or until surface appears set. Cool 30 minutes.
4. **For topping**, spread melted chocolate on top of brownie layer; garnish with pecans. Cool completely.

Tip: Bars may be made ahead and frozen in an airtight container for several weeks.

DEEP DISH APPLE COBBLER

12 to 16 servings

CRUST AND TOPPING
- 1 package Duncan Hines® Moist Deluxe Yellow Cake Mix
- 1 cup quick-cooking oats
- 1 cup chopped walnuts
- ¾ cup butter or margarine, melted

FILLING
- 7½ cups peeled and sliced apples (about 6 large)
- ½ cup raisins
- ½ cup water
- 3 tablespoons sugar
- 2 teaspoons ground cinnamon
- ½ teaspoon ground nutmeg

1. Preheat oven to 350°F. Grease and flour 13 × 9 × 2-inch pan.
2. **For crust and topping**, stir together cake mix, oats, walnuts and melted butter in large bowl. Sprinkle half of mixture into pan.
3. **For filling**, combine apples, raisins, water, sugar, cinnamon and nutmeg in large saucepan. Stir occasionally over low heat for 10 minutes. Spread filling over crust in pan. Sprinkle remaining topping mixture over filling. Bake at 350°F for 35 minutes or until lightly browned. Serve warm or at room temperature.

Tip: For a quick and easy preparation, apple filling can be heated in the microwave oven. Place filling ingredients in microwave-safe bowl and microwave at HIGH (100% power) for 6 minutes, stirring once.

Toffee Brownie Bars

DANISH ORANGE LOAVES

24 slices

CAKE

1 package Duncan Hines® Moist Deluxe Orange Supreme Cake Mix
1 package (4-serving size) vanilla instant pudding and pie filling mix
4 eggs
1 cup dairy sour cream
⅓ cup Crisco® Oil or Puritan® Oil

FROSTING

2¼ cups confectioners sugar
3 tablespoons butter or margarine, melted
2 to 3 tablespoons Citrus Hill® Orange Juice
1 tablespoon grated orange peel

1. Preheat oven to 350°F. Grease and flour two 9 × 5 × 3-inch loaf pans.
2. **For cake,** combine cake mix, pudding mix, eggs, sour cream and oil in large bowl. Beat at medium speed with electric mixer for 3 minutes. Pour batter into pans. Bake at 350°F for 50 to 60 minutes or until toothpick inserted in center comes out clean. Cool in pans 15 minutes. Loosen loaves from pan. Invert onto cooling rack. Turn right side up. Cool completely.
3. **For frosting,** combine confectioners sugar, melted butter and 1 tablespoon orange juice in small bowl. Beat at low speed with electric mixer until blended. Add remaining juice, 1 teaspoon at a time, until frosting is spreading consistency. Fold in orange peel. Spread frosting over cooled loaves.

Tip: This recipe may also be baked in a 10-inch Bundt® pan or tube pan for 50 to 60 minutes or until toothpick inserted comes out clean.

CHOCOLATE CARAMEL BARS

20 to 24 bars

1 package Duncan Hines® Moist Deluxe Swiss Chocolate Cake Mix
1 package (14 ounces) caramels
¾ cup butter or margarine
1 can (5 ounces) evaporated milk
1 cup chopped pecans
1 package (6 ounces) semi-sweet chocolate chips

1. Preheat oven to 350°F. Grease and flour 13 × 9 × 2-inch pan.
2. Prepare cake mix following package directions. Pour half of batter into pan. Bake at 350°F for 15 minutes.
3. Combine caramels, butter and evaporated milk in small saucepan. Cook over low heat until caramels are melted. Stir in pecans. Pour over hot baked layer. Sprinkle with chocolate chips. Spread remaining cake batter over top. Bake at 350°F for 35 to 45 minutes. Cool completely.

Tip: Cake will not test done with toothpick. Bake until top looks dry or press cake gently with your fingertip. Cake is done if it springs back.

Danish Orange Loaves

PEACHY CINNAMON COFFEECAKE

9 servings

1 package Duncan Hines® Bakery Style Cinnamon Swirl with Crumb Topping Muffin Mix
1 can (8¼ ounces) juice pack sliced yellow cling peaches
1 egg

1. Preheat oven to 400°F. Grease 8-inch square or 9-inch round pan.
2. Drain peaches, reserving juice. Add water to reserved juice to equal ¾ cup liquid. Chop peaches.
3. Combine muffin mix, egg and ¾ cup peach liquid in medium bowl; fold in peaches. Pour batter into pan. Knead swirl packet 10 seconds before opening. Squeeze contents on top of batter and swirl with knife. Sprinkle topping over batter. Bake at 400°F for 28 to 33 minutes for 8-inch pan (or 20 to 25 minutes for 9-inch pan) or until golden. Serve warm.

Tip: To test the freshness of your eggs, place them in a bowl of cold water. A fresh egg will sink; a stale egg will float.

MILK CHOCOLATE CHEESECAKE

8 servings

1 package Duncan Hines® Moist Deluxe Fudge Marble Cake Mix, divided
2 packages (8 ounces each) cream cheese, softened
8 ounces milk chocolate, melted
3 eggs
⅔ cup whipping cream
¼ cup plus 1 tablespoon butter or margarine, melted
Whipped cream, for garnish
Fresh strawberries, for garnish

1. Preheat oven to 350°F. Grease and flour 13 × 9 × 2-inch pan.
2. **For filling,** combine cocoa packet, ¼ cup dry cake mix, cream cheese and melted chocolate in large bowl. Beat at high speed with electric mixer for 2 minutes. Add eggs and cream. Beat 1 minute at high speed.
3. **For crust,** stir remaining dry cake mix and melted butter in medium bowl. Mixture will be crumbly. Sprinkle mixture into pan. Pour filling over crust mixture. Bake at 350°F for 30 to 35 minutes. Cool in pan. Refrigerate until chilled. Garnish each serving with whipped cream and strawberries.

Tip: Cheesecake may be soft in the center, but will become firm as it chills.

Peachy Cinnamon Coffeecake

SOUTHERN PECAN CAKE

12 servings

1 package Duncan Hines® Moist Deluxe French Vanilla Cake Mix
2 cups pecan pieces
1 package (4-serving size) vanilla instant pudding and pie filling mix
4 eggs
1 cup water
⅓ cup Crisco® Oil or Puritan® Oil
1 container (16 ounces) Duncan Hines® Cream Cheese Frosting

1. Preheat oven to 350°F. Grease and flour two 9-inch round cake pans.
2. Toast pecans on baking sheet at 350°F for 4 to 5 minutes or until fragrant. Cool. Chop finely. Measure 1½ cups. Reserve remaining pecans for garnish.
3. Combine cake mix, pudding mix, eggs, water and oil in large bowl. Beat at medium speed with electric mixer for 2 minutes. Fold in 1½ cups pecans. Pour into pans. Bake at 350°F for 35 to 40 minutes or until toothpick inserted in center comes out clean. Cool in pans 15 minutes. Invert onto cooling rack. Cool completely.
4. Fill and frost cake with cream cheese frosting. Garnish with reserved pecans. Refrigerate until ready to serve.

Tip: For a festive presentation, cut a 6-inch circle from waxed paper. Lay lightly on center of frosted cake. Sprinkle nuts around edge. Remove circle.

RASPBERRY-GLAZED BROWNIES

24 brownies

1 package Duncan Hines® Brownies Plus Milk Chocolate Chunks Mix
1 square (1 ounce) unsweetened chocolate, melted
2 tablespoons butter or margarine, softened
2 tablespoons light corn syrup
1 cup confectioners sugar
1 tablespoon milk
1 teaspoon vanilla extract
2 tablespoons seedless red raspberry jam

1. Preheat oven to 350°F. Grease and flour 13 × 9 × 2-inch pan. Prepare, bake and cool brownies following package directions.
2. Combine melted chocolate, butter and corn syrup in medium bowl. Stir in confectioners sugar, milk and vanilla extract. Add raspberry jam; mix well. Spread on top of cooled brownies.

Tip: For delicious flavor variations, use your favorite jam or preserves, such as orange marmalade, apricot or strawberry preserves.

Southern Pecan Cake

CHOCOLATE ALMOND COCONUT BARS

24 bars

- 1 package Duncan Hines® Moist Deluxe Devil's Food Cake Mix
- 1 package (6 ounces) slivered almonds, chopped
- ½ cup butter or margarine, melted
- 1½ cups flaked coconut, packed
- 3 eggs
- 1 cup semi-sweet mini chocolate chips

1. Preheat oven to 350°F. Toast almonds on baking sheet at 350°F about 5 minutes or until fragrant and light golden brown. Cool completely.
2. Combine cake mix, toasted almonds and melted butter in medium bowl. Press mixture into bottom of ungreased 13 × 9 × 2-inch pan.
3. Combine coconut and eggs in medium bowl. Stir with spoon until well blended. Spread over crust. Sprinkle with mini chocolate chips. Bake at 350°F for 20 to 25 minutes. Cool completely. Refrigerate until well chilled.

Tip: For a frosted look, try spreading the chocolate chips while still warm.

BLUEBERRY SOUR CREAM COFFEECAKE

9 servings

COFFEECAKE
- 1 package Duncan Hines® Blueberry Muffin Mix
- ⅓ cup dairy sour cream
- ¼ cup milk
- 1 egg
- ¼ cup blueberry preserves

GLAZE
- ½ cup confectioners sugar
- 2½ teaspoons water

1. Preheat oven to 375°F. Grease 8- or 9-inch round cake or pie pan.
2. Rinse blueberries with cold water and drain.
3. **For coffeecake,** combine dry muffin mix, sour cream, milk and egg in medium bowl. Stir until ingredients are moistened. Spread half of batter into pan.
4. Combine blueberries and preserves in small bowl. Spread half of blueberry mixture on top of batter. Spread remaining batter over blueberry layer. Spread remaining fruit on top, avoiding edges. Bake at 375°F for 30 to 35 minutes for 8-inch pan (or 25 to 30 minutes for 9-inch pan) or until golden.
5. **For glaze,** combine confectioners sugar and water in small bowl; stir until smooth. Drizzle over hot coffeecake.

Tip: Every time you open the oven door, the temperature will drop 25 to 30°F. Bake minimum time before checking for doneness.

LEMON MERINGUE TORTE

12 to 16 servings

1 package Duncan Hines® Moist Deluxe Lemon Supreme Cake Mix
1 package (4-serving size) lemon pudding and pie filling mix (not instant)
2 egg whites
¼ cup sugar

1. Preheat oven to 350°F. Grease and flour 15½ × 10½ × 1-inch jelly roll pan.
2. Prepare cake following package directions. Bake 25 to 30 minutes or until toothpick inserted in center comes out clean. Cool and remove from pan as directed on package.
3. Cook pudding mix as directed for pie filling. Cool 30 minutes. Stir several times.
4. **For meringue**, beat egg whites in small bowl at high speed with electric mixer until frothy. Add sugar gradually. Beat until stiff but not dry.
5. Reheat oven to 450°F.
6. Cut cake into thirds on 15½-inch side (5 inches wide). Place one layer on baking pan or oven-proof plate. Spread with pudding. Repeat. Reserve enough pudding for top of cake. Spread meringue around sides of cake. Bake at 450°F for 5 minutes or until light brown. Cool to room temperature before serving. Store in refrigerator.

Tip: To cool pudding quickly, place pan of cooked pudding in bowl of ice cubes; stir occasionally.

CHOCOLATE OAT CHEWIES

4½ dozen

1 package Duncan Hines® Moist Deluxe Devil's Food Cake Mix
1⅓ cups old-fashioned oats
1 cup flaked coconut, toasted and divided
¾ cup butter or margarine, melted
2 eggs, beaten
1 teaspoon vanilla extract
5 bars (1.55 ounces each) milk chocolate, cut into rectangles

1. Preheat oven to 350°F.
2. Combine cake mix, oats, ½ cup coconut, melted butter, eggs and vanilla extract in large bowl. Cover and chill 15 minutes.
3. Shape dough into 1-inch balls. Place balls 2 inches apart on ungreased baking sheet. Bake at 350°F for 12 minutes or until tops are slightly cracked. Remove from oven. Press one milk chocolate rectangle into center of each cookie. Sprinkle with remaining ½ cup coconut. Remove to cooling rack.

Tip: To toast coconut, spread on cookie sheet and bake at 350°F for 3 minutes. Stir and bake 1 to 2 minutes longer or until light golden brown.

FRENCH VANILLA BRICKLE CAKE

12 servings

CAKE
1 package Duncan Hines® Moist Deluxe French Vanilla Cake Mix
1 package (4-serving size) vanilla instant pudding and pie filling mix
4 eggs
½ cup sweetened condensed milk
½ cup butter or margarine, softened
½ cup almond brickle chips (reserve 2 teaspoons for garnish)

GLAZE
½ cup confectioners sugar
1 tablespoon brown sugar
1 tablespoon milk

1. Preheat oven to 350°F. Grease generously and flour 10-inch Bundt® pan.
2. **For cake,** combine cake mix, pudding mix, eggs, sweetened condensed milk and butter in large bowl. Beat at medium speed with electric mixer for 2 minutes. Fold in brickle chips. Pour into pan. Bake at 350°F for 50 to 60 minutes or until toothpick inserted in center comes out clean. Cool in pan 25 minutes. Invert onto serving plate. Cool completely.
3. **For glaze,** combine confectioners sugar and brown sugar in small bowl. Stir in milk until blended. Drizzle over cake. Sprinkle with reserved 2 teaspoons almond brickle chips.

Tip: For best results, have all cake ingredients at room temperature before you prepare the batter.

Chocolate Oat Chewies

CITRUS CROWN CAKE

12 servings

1 package Duncan Hines® Moist Deluxe Lemon Supreme Cake Mix
1 jar (12 ounces) orange marmalade
⅔ cup flaked coconut
¼ cup butter or margarine, melted

1. Preheat oven to 350°F. Grease generously and flour 10-inch Bundt® pan.
2. Combine marmalade, coconut and melted butter in small mixing bowl. Pour into pan.
3. Prepare cake following package directions. Pour batter over marmalade mixture. Bake at 350°F for 50 to 55 minutes or until toothpick inserted in center comes out clean. Cool in pan 10 minutes. Invert cake onto serving plate. Cool completely.

Tip: For best results, cut cake with a serrated knife; clean knife after each slice.

CHOCOLATE CHIP LAYER CAKE

12 to 16 servings

CAKE
1 package Duncan Hines® Moist Deluxe Yellow Cake Mix
1 package (4-serving size) vanilla instant pudding and pie filling mix
4 eggs
1 cup dairy sour cream
½ cup Crisco® Oil or Puritan® Oil
1 package (6 ounces) semi-sweet chocolate chips
1 square (1 ounce) unsweetened chocolate, grated
½ cup chopped pecans

FILLING AND FROSTING
2 cups whipped topping, divided
1 container (16 ounces) Duncan Hines® Chocolate Frosting
Pecan halves, for garnish (optional)

1. Preheat oven to 350°F. Grease and flour three 9-inch round cake pans.
2. **For cake,** combine cake mix, pudding mix, eggs, sour cream and oil. Beat at medium speed with electric mixer for 2 minutes. Stir in chocolate chips, grated chocolate and pecans. Pour batter into pans. Bake at 350°F for 35 to 40 minutes or until toothpick inserted in center comes out clean. Cool in pans 15 minutes. Remove from pans; cool completely.
3. **For filling,** spread 1 cup whipped topping on one cake layer. Place second cake layer on top of filling, spread with remaining 1 cup whipped topping; place third cake layer on top. Frost sides and top with chocolate frosting. Garnish with pecans halves, if desired. Refrigerate until ready to serve.

Tip: You can bake this cake in a greased and floured 10-inch Bundt® pan or tube pan for 50 to 60 minutes or until toothpick inserted in center comes out clean. Dust with confectioners sugar when cooled.

Citrus Crown Cake

CHOCOLATE CHIP RASPBERRY JUMBLES

16 bars

1 package Duncan Hines® Chocolate Chip Cookie Mix
½ cup seedless red raspberry preserves

1. Preheat oven to 350°F.
2. Prepare chocolate chip cookie mix following package directions. Reserve ½ cup dough.
3. Spread remaining dough into ungreased 9-inch square pan. Spread preserves over base. Drop teaspoonfuls of reserved dough randomly over top. Bake at 350°F for 20 to 25 minutes or until golden brown.

Tip: For delicious flavor variations, try strawberry or blackberry preserves.

LEMON CHEESE COFFEECAKE

16 to 20 servings

CAKE
1 package Duncan Hines® Moist Deluxe Lemon Supreme Cake Mix, divided
2 eggs
1 cup all-purpose flour
1 package active dry yeast
⅔ cup warm water

FILLING
2 packages (8 ounces each) cream cheese, softened
2 eggs
¼ cup sugar
1 tablespoon all-purpose flour
1 tablespoon milk

TOPPING
¼ cup plus 2 tablespoons butter or margarine, softened

GLAZE
1 cup confectioners sugar
1 tablespoon corn syrup
1 tablespoon water

1. Preheat oven to 350°F. Grease 13 × 9 × 2-inch pan.
2. **For cake,** combine 1½ cups cake mix, 2 eggs, 1 cup flour, yeast and ⅔ cup warm water in large bowl. Beat at medium speed with electric mixer for 2 minutes. Spread batter in pan.
3. **For filling,** combine cream cheese, 2 eggs, sugar, 1 tablespoon flour and milk in small bowl. Beat at low speed with electric mixer until blended. Spoon filling to cover batter.
4. **For topping,** mix remaining cake mix and butter until crumbly. Sprinkle over cheese filling. Bake at 350°F for 40 to 45 minutes or until golden brown. Cool completely.
5. **For glaze,** combine confectioners sugar, corn syrup and 1 tablespoon water in small bowl until smooth. Drizzle over hot coffeecake.

Tip: Also delicious using Duncan Hines® Moist Deluxe Yellow Cake Mix. Substitute 1 tablespoon lemon juice for the 1 tablespoon milk in filling.

Chocolate Chip Raspberry Jumbles

CHOCOLATE ALMOND CRUNCH CAKE

12 servings

CAKE
- 1 package Duncan Hines® Moist Deluxe Swiss Chocolate Cake Mix
- 1¼ cups natural chopped almonds, divided
- 3 eggs
- 1¼ cups water
- ¾ cup flaked coconut, divided
- ½ cup Crisco® Oil or Puritan® Oil
- 2 bars (1.55 ounces each) milk chocolate, melted

FROSTING
- 1 cup butter or margarine, chilled and cut into pieces
- 1 cup confectioners sugar, sifted
- 4 bars (1.55 ounces each) milk chocolate, melted

1. Preheat oven to 350°F. Grease and flour two 9-inch round cake pans.
2. Toast almonds in 350°F oven on baking sheet for 6 to 8 minutes or until fragrant and light golden brown. Cool completely.
3. **For cake,** combine cake mix, ½ cup toasted almonds, eggs, water, ½ cup coconut, oil and 2 melted chocolate bars in large mixing bowl. Prepare, bake and cool cake following package directions.
4. **For frosting,** combine butter, confectioners sugar and 4 melted chocolate bars in medium bowl. Beat at high speed with electric mixer for 3 minutes. Place one cake layer on serving plate. Spread with 1 cup frosting. Sprinkle with ½ cup toasted almonds. Top with second cake layer. Frost sides and top with remaining frosting. Garnish with ¼ cup coconut and ¼ cup toasted almonds. Refrigerate leftovers.

Tip: The frosting becomes firm when chilled. To cut cake easily, let cake stand 1 hour at room temperature before serving.

TRIPLE CHOCOLATE COOKIES

3½ to 4 dozen cookies

- 1 package Duncan Hines® Moist Deluxe Swiss Chocolate Cake Mix
- ½ cup butter or margarine, melted
- 1 egg
- ½ cup semi-sweet chocolate chips
- ½ cup milk chocolate chips
- ½ cup coarsely chopped white chocolate
- ½ cup chopped pecans

1. Preheat oven to 375°F.
2. Combine cake mix, melted butter and egg in large bowl. Stir in all 3 chocolates and pecans.
3. Drop by rounded tablespoonfuls onto ungreased baking sheets. Bake at 375°F for 9 to 11 minutes. Cool 1 minute on baking sheet. Remove to cooling rack.

Tip: Cookies may be stored in an airtight container in freezer for up to 6 months.

Chocolate Almond Crunch Cake

RICH PUMPKIN CHEESECAKE

8 to 12 servings

CRUST
- 1 package Duncan Hines® Moist Deluxe Spice Cake Mix
- ½ cup butter or margarine, melted

FILLING
- 3 packages (8 ounces each) cream cheese, softened
- 1 can (14 ounces) sweetened condensed milk
- 1 can (16 ounces) solid pack pumpkin
- 4 eggs
- 1 tablespoon pumpkin pie spice

TOPPING
- 1 package (2½ ounces) sliced almonds
- 2 cups whipping cream, chilled
- ¼ cup sugar

1. Preheat oven to 375°F.
2. **For crust,** combine cake mix and melted butter in large bowl; press into bottom of ungreased 10-inch springform pan.
3. **For filling,** combine cream cheese and sweetened condensed milk in large bowl. Beat with electric mixer at high speed for 2 minutes. Add pumpkin, eggs and pumpkin pie spice. Beat at high speed 1 minute. Pour over prepared crust in pan. Bake at 375°F for 65 to 70 minutes or until set. Cool completely on rack. Refrigerate 2 hours. Loosen cake from sides of pan; remove sides of pan.
4. **For topping,** preheat oven to 300°F. Toast almonds on baking sheet at 300°F 4 to 5 minutes or until fragrant and light golden brown. Cool completely. Beat cream in medium bowl until soft peaks form. Gradually add sugar; beat until stiff peaks form. Spread over top of chilled cake. Garnish with toasted almonds. Refrigerate until ready to serve.

Tip: To prepare in a 13 × 9 × 2-inch pan, bake at 350°F for 35 minutes or until set.

Rich Pumpkin Cheesecake

LEMON CRANBERRY LOAVES

24 slices

- 1 package Duncan Hines® Moist Deluxe Lemon Supreme Cake Mix
- 1¼ cups finely chopped fresh cranberries
- ½ cup finely chopped walnuts
- ¼ cup sugar
- 1 package (3 ounces) cream cheese, softened
- ¾ cup milk
- 4 eggs
- Confectioners sugar

1. Preheat oven to 350°F. Grease and flour two 8½ × 4½-inch loaf pans.
2. Stir together cranberries, walnuts and sugar in large bowl; set aside.
3. Combine cake mix, cream cheese and milk in large bowl. Beat at medium speed with electric mixer for 2 minutes. Add eggs, one at a time, beating for an additional 2 minutes. Fold in cranberry mixture. Pour into pans. Bake at 350°F for 45 to 50 minutes or until toothpick inserted in center comes out clean. Cool in pans 15 minutes. Loosen loaves from pans. Invert onto cooling rack. Turn right side up. Cool completely. Dust with confectioners sugar.

Tip: To quickly chop cranberries or walnuts, use a food processor fitted with the steel blade and pulse until evenly chopped.

PUMPKIN STREUSEL CAKE

16 to 20 servings

STREUSEL

- ⅓ cup butter or margarine
- 1 cup firmly packed brown sugar
- 2 teaspoons ground cinnamon
- 1 cup chopped nuts

CAKE

- 1 package Duncan Hines® Moist Deluxe Yellow Cake Mix
- 1 can (16 ounces) solid pack pumpkin
- 3 eggs
- 1 cup dairy sour cream
- ½ cup butter or margarine, softened

1. Preheat oven to 350°F.
2. **For streusel,** cut ⅓ cup butter into brown sugar and cinnamon using pastry blender or 2 knives. Stir in chopped nuts. Set aside.
3. **For cake,** combine cake mix, pumpkin, eggs, sour cream and ½ cup butter in large bowl. Beat at medium speed with electric mixer for 2 minutes. Spread half of batter into 13 × 9 × 2 inch pan. Sprinkle half of streusel over batter. Spread remaining batter over streusel. Top with remaining streusel. Bake at 350°F for 50 to 55 minutes or until toothpick inserted in center comes out clean.

Tip: Serve warm as a coffeecake or cool as a dessert topped with whipped topping.

Lemon Cranberry Loaves

PUMPKIN PIE CRUNCH

16 to 20 servings

- 1 package Duncan Hines® Moist Deluxe Yellow Cake Mix
- 1 can (16 ounces) solid pack pumpkin
- 1 can (12 ounces) evaporated milk
- 3 eggs
- 1½ cups sugar
- 4 teaspoons pumpkin pie spice
- ½ teaspoon salt
- 1 cup chopped pecans
- 1 cup butter or margarine, melted
- Whipped topping

1. Preheat oven to 350°F. Grease bottom of 13 × 9 × 2-inch pan.
2. Combine pumpkin, evaporated milk, eggs, sugar, pumpkin pie spice and salt in large bowl. Pour into pan. Sprinkle dry cake mix evenly over pumpkin mixture. Top with pecans. Drizzle with melted butter. Bake at 350°F for 50 to 55 minutes or until golden. Cool completely. Serve with whipped topping. Refrigerate leftovers.

Tip: For a richer flavor, try using Duncan Hines® Moist Deluxe Butter Recipe Golden Cake Mix.

CRANBERRY ORANGE CAKE

16 servings

CAKE

- 1 package Duncan Hines® Moist Deluxe Orange Supreme Cake Mix
- 1 cup chopped dates
- 1 cup halved cranberries
- 1 cup finely chopped walnuts
- ½ cup all-purpose flour
- 1 package (4-serving size) vanilla instant pudding and pie filling mix
- 4 eggs
- 1 cup water
- ⅓ cup Crisco® Oil or Puritan® Oil
- 2 tablespoons grated orange peel

TOPPING

- ⅔ cup Citrus Hill® Orange Juice
- ⅔ cup sugar
- Whipped topping

1. Preheat oven to 350°F. Grease and flour 10-inch tube pan.
2. **For cake,** stir together dates, cranberries, walnuts and flour in medium bowl; set aside.
3. Combine cake mix, pudding mix, eggs, water and oil in large bowl. Beat at medium speed with electric mixer for 2 minutes. Stir in flour-coated dates, cranberries and walnuts with orange peel. Pour batter into pan. Bake at 350°F for about 60 minutes or until toothpick inserted in center comes out clean. Cool in pan 25 minutes. Invert onto serving plate.
4. **For topping,** combine orange juice and sugar in small saucepan. Heat until sugar is dissolved. Pour half of glaze over cake. Serve with remaining glaze and whipped topping.

Tip: To save preparation time, purchase dates that have already been chopped.

Pumpkin Pie Crunch

FRESH APPLE CAKE

12 to 16 servings

CAKE

1 package Duncan Hines® Moist Deluxe Yellow Cake Mix
3 eggs
1¼ cups apple juice
⅓ cup Crisco® Oil or Puritan® Oil
1 teaspoon ground cinnamon
2 cups grated apples (about 2 medium apples)
½ cup all-purpose flour
1 cup chopped pecans

FROSTING

3 tablespoons butter or margarine
3 tablespoons brown sugar
3 tablespoons granulated sugar
3 tablespoons whipping cream
½ cup confectioners sugar
¼ teaspoon vanilla extract

1. Preheat oven to 350°F. Grease and flour 10-inch tube pan.
2. **For cake**, combine cake mix, eggs, apple juice, oil and cinnamon in large bowl. Beat at medium speed with electric mixer for 2 minutes. Toss apples with flour in medium bowl. Fold flour-coated apples and pecans into batter. Pour into prepared pan. Bake at 350°F for 45 minutes or until toothpick inserted in center comes out clean. Cool in pan 25 minutes. Invert onto serving plate. Cool completely.
3. **For frosting**, combine butter, brown sugar, sugar and whipping cream in small heavy saucepan. Bring to a boil over medium heat; boil 1 minute. Remove from heat; cool 20 minutes. Add confectioners sugar and vanilla extract; blend with wooden spoon until smooth and thick. Spread frosting on cake.

Tip: Apples may be grated in a food processor fitted with the shredding disc. If a food processor is not available, use a hand grater.

CRANBERRY STRAWBERRY CAKE

16 to 20 servings

1 package Duncan Hines® Moist Deluxe Strawberry Supreme Cake Mix
1 container (12 ounces) cranberry-strawberry sauce
1 container (8 ounces) frozen whipped topping, thawed

1. Preheat oven to 350°F. Grease and flour 13 × 9 × 2-inch pan. Prepare, bake and cool cake following package directions.
2. Spread cranberry-strawberry sauce on top of cake. Frost with whipped topping. Refrigerate until ready to serve.

Tip: Garnish each serving with a fresh strawberry, if desired.

Fresh Apple Cake

PUMPKIN SPICE CAKE WITH PUMPKIN CREAM TOPPING

12 to 16 servings

CAKE
- 1 package Duncan Hines® Moist Deluxe Spice Cake Mix
- 2 eggs
- 1 cup water
- 1 can (16 ounces) solid pack pumpkin, divided
- 1 cup chopped nuts
- Confectioners sugar

TOPPING
- 1 container (8 ounces) frozen whipped topping, thawed
- 1 tablespoon sugar

1. Preheat oven to 350°F. Grease and flour 10-inch Bundt® pan.
2. **For cake,** combine cake mix, eggs, water and 1 cup pumpkin in large bowl. Beat at medium speed with electric mixer for 2 minutes. Stir in nuts. Pour into pan. Bake at 350°F for 40 to 50 minutes or until toothpick inserted in center comes out clean. Cool in pan 25 minutes. Invert onto serving plate. Cool completely. Dust with confectioners sugar.
3. **For topping,** mix together whipped topping, remaining ¾ cup pumpkin and sugar. Spoon over cake slices to serve.

Tip: To dust cake easily, place confectioners sugar in a small strainer and gently shake over cake.

BUTTERY CRANBERRY COBBLER

10 to 12 servings

- 1 package Duncan Hines® Moist Deluxe Butter Recipe Golden Cake Mix, divided
- 1 cup quick-cooking oats
- ¾ cup butter or margarine, softened and divided
- 2 eggs
- ⅓ cup water
- 1 can (16 ounces) whole berry cranberry sauce

1. Preheat oven to 375°F. Grease and flour 13 × 9 × 2-inch pan.
2. **For topping,** combine ½ cup dry cake mix, oats and ¼ cup butter in medium bowl with fork until crumbly. Set aside.
3. **For base,** cut together remaining dry cake mix and remaining ½ cup butter with fork until crumbly. Stir in eggs and water until mixture is moistened. Spread on bottom of pan.
4. Stir cranberry sauce until smooth. Spread over batter in pan. Sprinkle with topping. Bake at 375°F for 35 to 40 minutes or until toothpick inserted in center comes out clean. Cool 10 minutes before serving.

Tip: To quickly soften cold butter, place 1 unwrapped stick of butter in microwave oven and microwave at HIGH (100% power) for 10 seconds.

CRANBERRY ORANGE CHEESECAKE BARS

12 to 16 servings

1 package Duncan Hines® Bakery Style Cranberry Orange Nut with Crumb Topping Muffin Mix
¼ cup butter or margarine
1 package (8 ounces) cream cheese, softened
½ cup sugar
1 egg
3 tablespoons Citrus Hill® Orange Juice
½ teaspoon vanilla extract

1. Preheat oven to 350°F. Grease an 8- or 9-inch square pan.
2. Rinse cranberries with cold water and drain.
3. Cut butter into muffin mix with pastry blender or 2 knives in medium bowl. Press into bottom of pan. Bake at 350°F for 15 minutes.
4. Blend cream cheese and sugar until smooth in large bowl. Add egg, orange juice and vanilla extract. Beat well. Spread over baked crust. Sprinkle with cranberries. Sprinkle topping from packet over cranberries. Return to oven. Bake at 350°F for 35 to 40 minutes for 8-inch pan (or 30 to 35 minutes for 9-inch pan) or until filling is set. Cool completely. Refrigerate until ready to serve.

Tip: Lower oven temperature by 25°F when using glass baking dishes. Glass heats more quickly and retains heat longer.

SPICY MINCEMEAT COOKIES

5 dozen cookies

1 package Duncan Hines® Moist Deluxe Spice Cake Mix
2 eggs
⅓ cup Crisco® Oil or Puritan® Oil
½ package (9-ounce box) condensed mincemeat, crumbled
Confectioners sugar (optional)

1. Preheat oven to 400°F.
2. Combine cake mix, eggs and oil in large bowl. Stir in mincemeat.
3. Drop by rounded measuring teaspoonfuls onto ungreased baking sheet. Flatten slightly using the bottom of a glass. Bake at 400°F for 6 to 8 minutes or until lightly browned. Cool 1 minute on baking sheet. Remove to cooling rack. Dust cookies with confectioners sugar, if desired.

Tip: Refrigerate or freeze remaining mincemeat in an airtight container.

SPECIAL HONEYED FRUIT CAKE

12 to 16 servings

CAKE
- 1 package Duncan Hines® Moist Deluxe Butter Recipe Golden Cake Mix
- 6 egg whites
- ⅔ cup water
- ½ cup margarine, melted
- 1 tablespoon molasses
- 1 cup chopped nuts
- ½ cup raisins

SYRUP
- ¼ cup Citrus Hill® Orange Juice
- ¼ cup honey
- ¼ cup granulated sugar
- Juice and grated peel from 1 lemon
- ¼ teaspoon ground cinnamon

GLAZE
- ¾ cup confectioners sugar
- 2 tablespoons skim milk
- ½ teaspoon brandy
- Candied cherry halves
- Pecan halves

1. Preheat oven to 375°F. Grease and flour a 10-inch Bundt® pan.
2. **For cake**, combine cake mix, egg whites, water, melted margarine and molasses in large bowl. Beat at medium speed with electric mixer for 2 minutes. Fold in nuts and raisins. Pour into pan. Bake at 375°F for 35 to 40 minutes or until toothpick inserted in center comes out clean. Cool cake 10 minutes. Invert onto serving plate. Return cake to pan. Poke holes in cake 1-inch apart with a skewer or meat fork.
3. **For syrup**, combine all syrup ingredients in small saucepan over medium heat. Simmer 10 minutes, stirring occasionally. Pour hot syrup evenly over cake in pan. Cool cake completely before inverting onto serving plate.
4. **For glaze**, combine confectioners sugar, milk and brandy in small bowl. Beat until smooth. Drizzle over cooled cake. Garnish with candied cherries and pecans.

Tip: For variety, substitute currants or dates for raisins.

Special Honeyed Fruit Cake

CHERRY ANGEL ROLLS

16 to 20 servings

1 package Duncan Hines® Angel Food Cake Mix
1 cup chopped maraschino cherries, drained
½ cup flaked coconut
1 teaspoon maraschino cherry juice
1 container (8 ounces) frozen whipped topping, thawed
Confectioners sugar

1. Preheat oven to 350°F. Line two 15½ × 10½ × 1-inch jelly roll pans with aluminum foil.
2. Prepare cake following package directions. Divide batter into lined pans. Spread evenly. Cut through batter with knife or spatula to remove large air bubbles. Bake at 350°F for 15 minutes or until set. Immediately invert cakes onto towels covered with confectioners sugar. Remove foil carefully. Roll up each cake with towel jelly roll fashion. Cool completely.
3. Fold cherries, coconut and cherry juice into whipped topping. Unroll cakes. Spread half of filling over each cake to edges. Reroll and place seam-side down on serving plate. Dust with confectioners sugar. Refrigerate until ready to serve.

Tip: Use clean, lint-free dishtowels to roll up cakes.

APRICOT DESSERT CAKE

16 to 20 servings

CAKE
1 package Duncan Hines® Moist Deluxe White Cake Mix
3 egg whites
1¼ cups water
⅓ cup Puritan® Oil
½ cup finely chopped dried apricots

APRICOT SAUCE
1 can (16 ounces) unpeeled apricot halves, drained
¼ cup superfine sugar
2 tablespoons lemon juice

1. Preheat oven to 350°F. Grease and flour 13 × 9 × 2-inch pan.
2. **For cake**, combine cake mix, egg whites, water and oil in large bowl. Beat at medium speed with electric mixer for 2 minutes. Fold in finely chopped apricots. Pour into pan. Bake at 350°F for 30 to 35 minutes or until toothpick inserted in center comes out clean. Cool completely.
3. **For apricot sauce**, place apricot halves, sugar and lemon juice in blender or food processor fitted with the steel blade. Process until smooth. Pour sauce over cake slices to serve.

Tip: Use your food processor to quickly chop dried apricots. Combine ½ cup dry cake mix and apricots in work bowl fitted with the steel blade; process until finely chopped.

Cherry Angel Rolls

BANANA OATMEAL MUFFINS

12 large muffins

1 package Duncan Hines® Hearty Style Oatmeal with Apples & Walnuts Muffin Mix
2 egg whites
¾ cup water
1 medium-size ripe banana, mashed

1. Preheat oven to 400°F. Grease 2½-inch muffin cups (or use paper liners).
2. Empty muffin mix into bowl. Break up any lumps. Add egg whites, water and mashed banana until blended. Stir until moistened, about 50 strokes.
3. Bake and cool muffins following package directions.

Tip: Stir muffin batter with a wooden spoon; never use an electric mixer.

ORANGE WAKE UP CAKE

12 to 16 servings

CAKE
1 package Duncan Hines® Moist Deluxe Yellow Cake Mix
3 egg whites
1¼ cups water
⅓ cup Puritan® Oil
1 tablespoon grated orange peel

TOPPING
½ cup chopped pecans
⅓ cup firmly packed brown sugar
¼ cup fine graham cracker crumbs
2 tablespoons margarine, melted
1 tablespoon grated orange peel
1½ teaspoons ground cinnamon

GLAZE
1 cup confectioners sugar
2 tablespoons Citrus Hill® Orange Juice

1. Preheat oven to 375°F. Grease and flour two 9-inch round cake pans.
2. **For cake,** combine cake mix, egg whites, water and oil in large bowl. Beat at medium speed with electric mixer for 2 minutes. Fold in 1 tablespoon orange peel. Pour batter into pans.
3. **For topping,** combine chopped pecans, brown sugar, graham cracker crumbs, melted margarine, 1 tablespoon orange peel and cinnamon in medium bowl. Stir until well mixed. Sprinkle over batter in pans.
4. Bake at 375°F for 25 to 30 minutes or until toothpick inserted in center comes out clean.
5. **For glaze,** combine confectioners sugar and orange juice in small bowl; mix until smooth. Immediately pour glaze over baked layers. Serve warm or at room temperature.

Tip: Recipe makes 2 cakes. If you like, serve one immediately and freeze the other for a quick coffeecake at a later time. Freeze in resealable plastic bag. Cake can also be baked in 13 × 9 × 2-inch pan following package baking time.

Banana Oatmeal Muffins

FRENCH VANILLA FRUIT DELIGHT

12 servings

1 package Duncan Hines® Moist Deluxe French Vanilla Cake Mix
1 can (8¾ ounces) unpeeled apricot halves, drained
1 jar (12 ounces) apricot preserves

1. Preheat oven to 350°F. Grease and flour 10-inch tube pan. Prepare, bake and cool cake following package directions for no-cholesterol recipe.
2. Arrange apricot halves on top of cake. Heat apricot preserves until warm. Pour over apricot halves and cake. Refrigerate until ready to serve.

Tip: For a delicious flavor variation, substitute raspberry or strawberry preserves for apricot preserves.

LEMON ANGEL FOOD CAKE WITH BLUEBERRY SAUCE

12 to 16 servings

CAKE
1 package Duncan Hines® Angel Food Cake Mix
1 cup plus 3 tablespoons water
2 tablespoons lemon juice
Few drops yellow food coloring
1 teaspoon grated lemon peel

SAUCE
⅔ cup sugar
2 tablespoons cornstarch
⅛ teaspoon salt
⅔ cup water
2 cups frozen dry pack blueberries
Additional grated lemon peel, for garnish

1. Preheat oven to 375°F.
2. **For cake**, combine 1 cup plus 3 tablespoons water, lemon juice and yellow food coloring in small bowl. Mix Angel Food Cake following package directions except use water mixture for the 1⅓ cups water called for on the package. Add 1 teaspoon grated lemon peel and Cake Flour Mixture (red "B" packet). Bake and cool cake following package directions.
3. **For sauce**, combine sugar, cornstarch and salt in small saucepan. Stir in ⅔ cup water. Cook over medium heat, stirring constantly, until thickened. Remove from heat. Stir in frozen blueberries. Refrigerate until chilled.
4. Spoon chilled blueberry sauce on top of cake. If desired, reserve a small amount of sauce to spoon over individual cake slices. Garnish with additional grated lemon peel. Refrigerate until ready to serve.

French Vanilla Fruit Delight

BLUEBERRY ORANGE LOAF

12 slices

- 1 package Duncan Hines® Bakery Style Blueberry with Crumb Topping Muffin Mix
- ½ teaspoon baking powder
- 2 egg whites
- ⅔ cup Citrus Hill® Orange Juice
- 1 teaspoon grated orange peel

1. Preheat oven to 350°F. Grease one 8 × 4-inch or 9 × 5-inch loaf pan.
2. Rinse blueberries with cold water and drain.
3. Empty muffin mix into bowl. Add baking powder; stir to combine and break up any lumps. Add egg whites and orange juice. Stir until moistened, about 50 strokes. Fold in blueberries and orange peel. Pour into pan. Sprinkle topping from packet over batter. Bake at 350°F for 45 to 55 minutes or until toothpick inserted in center comes out clean. Cool in pan 10 minutes. Loosen loaf from pan. Invert onto cooling rack. Turn right side up. Cool completely.

Tip: Freeze extra grated orange peel for future use.

CHOCOLATE CHERRY ANGEL FOOD CAKE

12 servings

- 1 package Duncan Hines® Angel Food Cake Mix
- ½ cup finely chopped nuts
- ¼ cup finely chopped maraschino cherries, drained
- ¼ cup mini semi-sweet chocolate chips
- ½ cup Duncan Hines® Chocolate Frosting

1. Preheat oven to 375°F.
2. Combine nuts, cherries, chocolate chips and Cake Flour Mixture (red "B" packet) in large bowl. Prepare, bake and cool cake following package directions.
3. Heat frosting until thin. Glaze cake, allowing frosting to drizzle down sides. Garnish with cherries or nuts, if desired.

Tip: After chopping maraschino cherries, allow them to drain on paper towels.

Blueberry Orange Loaf

FUDGE CAKE WITH MELBA TOPPING

16 to 20 servings

CAKE
- 1 package Duncan Hines® Moist Deluxe Dark Dutch Fudge Cake Mix
- Egg substitute product equal to 3 eggs
- 1¼ cups water
- ½ cup Puritan® Oil

RASPBERRY SAUCE
- 1 package (12 ounces) frozen dry pack raspberries, thawed, drained and juice reserved
- ½ cup sugar
- 2 teaspoons cornstarch
- ½ teaspoon grated lemon peel

- 1 can (29 ounces) sliced peaches in heavy syrup, drained

1. Preheat oven to 350°F. Grease and flour 13 × 9 × 2-inch pan.
2. **For cake**, combine cake mix, egg substitute, water and oil in large bowl. Beat at medium speed with electric mixer for 2 minutes. Pour into pan. Bake at 350°F for 35 to 40 minutes or until toothpick inserted in center comes out clean. Cool completely.
3. **For sauce**, combine reserved raspberry juice, sugar, cornstarch and lemon peel in medium saucepan. Bring to a boil. Reduce heat and cook until thickened, stirring constantly. Stir in reserved raspberries. Cool.
4. Cut cake into serving squares. Place several peach slices on top of each cake square. Spoon raspberry sauce over peaches and cake. Serve immediately.

Tip: To separate juice from raspberries in one step, allow berries to thaw at room temperature in a strainer placed over a bowl.

BLUEBERRY STREUSEL COFFECAKE

16 to 20 servings

- 1 package Duncan Hines® Moist Deluxe Yellow Cake Mix, divided
- Egg substitute product equal to 2 eggs
- 1 cup all-purpose flour
- ⅔ cup warm water
- 1 package active dry yeast
- 1 can (21 ounces) blueberry pie filling
- ⅓ cup margarine, melted
- 2 tablespoons sugar

1. Preheat oven to 375°F. Grease 13 × 9 × 2-inch pan.
2. Combine 1½ cups cake mix, egg substitute, flour, water and yeast in large bowl. Beat at medium speed with electric mixer for 2 minutes. Spread dough in pan. Spoon pie filling over dough. Combine remaining cake mix and melted margarine in medium bowl. Sprinkle over pie filling. Sprinkle with sugar. Bake at 375°F for 30 to 35 minutes or until golden brown.

Tip: For a delicious flavor variation, try using cherry or peach pie filling.

Fudge Cake with Melba Topping

NUTTY BLUEBERRY MUFFINS

8 large or 12 medium muffins

- 1 package Duncan Hines® Blueberry Muffin Mix
- 2 egg whites
- ½ cup water
- ⅓ cup chopped pecans

1. Preheat oven to 400°F. Grease 2½-inch muffin cups (or use paper liners).
2. Rinse blueberries with cold water and drain.
3. Empty muffin mix into bowl. Break up any lumps. Add egg whites and water. Stir until moistened, about 50 strokes. Stir in nuts; fold in blueberries.
4. For large muffins, fill cups ⅔ full. Bake at 400°F for 17 to 22 minutes or until toothpick inserted in center comes out clean. For medium muffins, fill cups ½ full. Bake at 400°F for 15 to 20 minutes. Cool 5 to 10 minutes.

Tip: Use walnuts instead of pecans.

CHOCOLATY ORANGE CAKE

12 servings

CAKE

- 1 package Duncan Hines® Moist Deluxe Devil's Food Cake Mix
- Egg substitute product equal to 3 eggs
- 1⅓ cups Citrus Hill® Orange Juice
- ½ cup Puritan® Oil
- 1 teaspoon grated orange peel

GLAZE

- 1 cup sifted confectioners sugar
- 2 teaspoons margarine, softened
- 1 teaspoon grated orange peel
- 2 to 3 tablespoons Citrus Hill® Orange Juice

1. Preheat oven to 350°F. Grease and flour 10-inch Bundt® pan.
2. **For cake,** combine all cake ingredients in large bowl. Beat at medium speed with electric mixer for 2 minutes. Pour into pan. Bake at 350°F for 45 to 55 minutes or until toothpick inserted in center comes out clean. Cool in pan for 25 minutes. Invert onto serving plate. Cool completely.
3. **For glaze,** combine confectioners sugar, margarine and 1 teaspoon orange peel in small bowl. Add orange juice, 1 tablespoon at a time, until glaze is spreading consistency. Spoon over cake.

Tip: Use a clean toothbrush to remove excess orange peel from your grater.

Nutty Blueberry Muffins

JACK-O-LANTERN CAKE

12 to 16 servings

1 package Duncan Hines® Moist Deluxe Cake Mix (any flavor)
2 containers (16 ounces) Duncan Hines® Vanilla Frosting, divided
1 flat bottom ice cream cone
Green, red and yellow food coloring

1. Preheat oven to 375°F. Grease and flour 10-inch Bundt® pan. Prepare, bake and cool cake following package directions.
2. Measure ¼ cup frosting into small bowl. Tint with green food coloring. Place ice cream cone upside down on waxed paper. Frost with green frosting. Refrigerate.
3. Tint remaining frosting with red and yellow food coloring until frosting is desired orange color. Measure 3 tablespoons orange frosting in small bowl; add green food coloring to make brown frosting.
4. Frost cake with orange frosting. Make eyes, mouth and nose with brown frosting as desired on pumpkin. Place green frosted ice cream cone in center hole of cake for stem.

Tip: Decorate serving plate with green-tinted coconut.

Jack-O-Lantern Cake

VALENTINE PARTY CUPCAKES

24 cupcakes

1 package Duncan Hines® Moist Deluxe Strawberry Supreme Cake Mix
1 container (16 ounces) Duncan Hines® Polka Dot Pink Vanilla Frosting
Assorted valentine candies, for garnish
Cinnamon candy hearts, for garnish

1. Preheat oven to 350°F. Place 2½-inch paper liners in 24 muffin cups. Prepare, bake and cool cupcakes following package directions.
2. Frost cupcakes with pink vanilla frosting. Decorate with assorted valentine candies and cinnamon hearts.

Tip: Make Halloween party cupcakes by using any Duncan Hines® Moist Deluxe Chocolate Cake Mix and frost with Duncan Hines® Chocolate Frosting. Decorate with candy corn and candy pumpkins.

CHOCOLATE PEANUT BUTTER CUPCAKES

24 cupcakes

1 package Duncan Hines® Moist Deluxe Cake Mix, any chocolate flavor
1½ cups Jif® Peanut Butter
¾ cup chopped peanuts

1. Preheat oven to 350°F. Place 2½-inch paper liners in 24 muffin cups. Prepare, bake and cool cupcakes following package directions.
2. Stir peanut butter to soften. Spread 1 tablespoon on top of each cupcake. Dip in chopped peanuts.

Tip: To make Snowball Cupcakes, frost with Duncan Hines® Vanilla Frosting. Sprinkle with flaked coconut.

Valentine Party Cupcakes

TAKES
TWO TO
TANGO

STAR CHRISTMAS TREE COOKIES

2 to 3 dozen cookies

COOKIES
1 package Duncan Hines® Moist Deluxe Yellow or Devil's Food Cake Mix
½ cup Crisco® Shortening
⅓ cup butter or margarine, softened
2 egg yolks
1 teaspoon vanilla extract
1 tablespoon water

FROSTING
1 container (16 ounces) Duncan Hines® Vanilla Frosting
Green food coloring
Red and green sugar crystals, for garnish
Assorted colored candies and decors, for garnish

1. Preheat oven to 375°F.
2. **For cookies,** combine shortening, butter, egg yolks and vanilla extract. Blend in cake mix gradually. Add 1 teaspoonful water at a time until dough is rolling consistency. Divide dough into 4 balls. Flatten one ball with hand; roll to ⅛-inch thickness on lightly floured surface. Cut with graduated sized star cookie cutters. Repeat using remaining dough. Bake large cookies together on ungreased baking sheet at 375°F for 6 to 8 minutes or until edges are light golden brown. Cool cookies 1 minute. Remove from baking sheet. Repeat with smaller cookies, testing for doneness at minimum bake time.
3. **For frosting,** tint vanilla frosting with green food coloring. Frost cookies and stack beginning with largest cookies on bottom and ending with smallest cookies on top. Rotate cookies when stacking to alternate corners. Decorate as desired with colored sugar crystals and assorted colored candies and decors.

Tip: If assorted star cutters are not available, use your favorite assorted cookie cutters. Stack cookies into one large "tree" or stack into smaller trees using 3 to 5 cookies per tree.

Star Christmas Tree Cookies

BROWNIE PIZZA

12 servings

1 package Duncan Hines® Brownies Plus Milk Chocolate Chunks Mix
1 egg
⅓ cup Crisco® Oil or Puritan® Oil
2 tablespoons water
Vanilla ice cream
Strawberry slices
Kiwi wedges
Pineapple chunks
Apricot halves
Chocolate syrup

1. Preheat oven to 350°F. Grease 13-inch round pizza pan.
2. Combine brownie mix, egg, oil and water in large bowl. Stir with spoon until well blended, about 50 strokes. Spread in pan. Bake at 350°F for 23 to 27 minutes. Cool completely.
3. Cut into wedges, top with scoops of ice cream, decorate with assorted fruit, then drizzle with chocolate syrup.

Tip: For convenience, purchase pre-cut fruit from the salad bar at your local grocery store.

SURPRISE COOKIES

2 to 3 dozen

1 package Duncan Hines® Golden Sugar Cookie Mix
1 egg
Miniature gum drops
Candy coated chocolate
Candied cherries
Chocolate stars
Whole pecans, walnuts or almonds

1. Preheat oven to 375°F.
2. Combine dry cookie mix, butter flavor packet and egg in large bowl. Stir until thoroughly blended.
3. Shape thin layer of dough around desired filling. Place 2 inches apart on ungreased baking sheet. Bake at 375°F for 7 minutes or until set but not browned. Cool 1 minute on baking sheet. Remove to cooling rack. Cool completely. Dust with confectioners sugar.

Tip: Stir dry cookie mix with fork to break up lumps before adding butter flavor packet and egg.

Brownie Pizza

FOOTBALL CAKE

12 to 16 servings

1 package Duncan Hines® Moist Deluxe Devil's Food Cake Mix

DECORATOR FROSTING

¾ cup confectioners sugar
2 tablespoons Crisco® Shortening
1 tablespoon cold water
1 tablespoon non-dairy creamer
¼ teaspoon vanilla extract
Dash salt

1 container (16 ounces) Duncan Hines® Chocolate Frosting

1. Preheat oven to 350°F. Grease and flour 10-inch round cake pan. Prepare cake following package directions. Bake at 350°F for 45 to 55 minutes or until toothpick inserted in center comes out clean.

2. **For decorator frosting,** combine confectioners sugar, shortening, water, non-dairy creamer, vanilla extract and salt in small bowl. Beat at medium speed with electric mixer for 2 minutes. Beat at high speed for 3 minutes. Add more confectioners sugar to thicken or water to thin frosting as needed.

3. Cut cake and remove 2-inch slice from center. Arrange cake as shown. Spread chocolate frosting on sides and top of cake. Place basketweave tip in pastry bag. Fill with decorator frosting. Make white frosting laces on football.

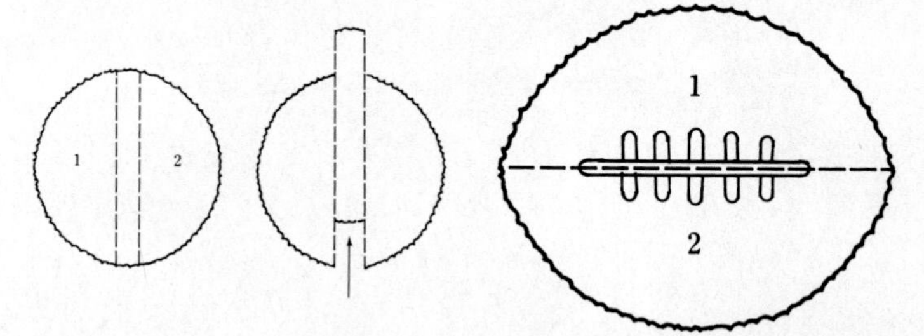

Tip: If a 10-inch round pan is not available, make 2 football cakes by following package directions for baking with two 9-inch round cake pans.

Football Cake

GINGERBREAD MEN

12 to 14 six-inch tall gingerbread men

1 package Duncan Hines® Moist Deluxe Spice Cake Mix
½ cup all-purpose flour
2 eggs
⅓ cup Crisco® Oil or Puritan® Oil
⅓ cup dark molasses
2 teaspoons ground ginger
Raisins for decorations

1. Combine cake mix, flour, eggs, oil, molasses and ginger in large bowl (mixture will be soft). Refrigerate 2 hours.
2. Preheat oven to 375°F.
3. Roll dough to ¼-inch thickness on lightly floured surface. Cut with gingerbread man cookie cutter. Place on ungreased baking sheet 3 inches apart. Decorate with raisins.
4. Bake at 375°F for 8 to 10 minutes or until edges start to brown. Remove immediately to cooling rack.

Tip: To make holes for hanging cookie ornaments, push straw or meat skewer in head section of cookies before baking.

BERRY BARS

1½ dozen bars

1 package Duncan Hines® Blueberry Muffin Mix
1 cup old-fashioned oats
¼ cup firmly packed brown sugar
¼ cup plus 2 tablespoons butter or margarine
½ cup raspberry preserves

1. Preheat oven to 375°F. Grease 8-inch square pan.
2. Rinse blueberries with cold water and drain.
3. Combine dry muffin mix, oats and sugar in large bowl. Cut in butter using pastry blender or 2 knives; reserve 1½ cups. Press remaining crumb mixture in pan.
4. Fold blueberries into jam. Spread on top of crumb mixture. Sprinkle with 1½ cups reserved crumbs. Pat evenly on berry mixture. Bake at 375°F for 20 to 25 minutes or until golden. Cool completely. Cut into bars.

Tip: Blackberry jam can be substituted for raspberry preserves.

Gingerbread Men

Duncan Hines®

Index

Save on

MANUFACTURER COUPON | NO EXPIRATION DATE

87968

SAVE 20¢

when you buy Duncan Hines Sheetcake Frosting

PROCTER & GAMBLE

87968

MANUFACTURER COUPON | NO EXPIRATION DATE

87981

SAVE 20¢

when you buy Duncan Hines Angel Food Cake Mix

(or three any other Duncan Hines Cake Mixes)

PROCTER & GAMBLE

87981

Save on

MANUFACTURER COUPON | NO EXPIRATION DATE

87968

SAVE 20¢

when you buy Duncan Hines Sheetcake Frosting

PROCTER & GAMBLE

CONSUMER: Redeem ONLY by purchasing the brand size(s) indicated. May not be reproduced. Void if transferred to any person, firm or group prior to store redemption. You pay any sales tax. Any other use constitutes fraud. **LIMIT ONE COUPON PER PURCHASE.**
DEALER: Sending coupons to **Procter & Gamble,** 2150 Sunnybrook Drive, Cincinnati, Ohio 45237 signifies compliance with "Requirements for Proper Coupon Redemption." Copy available by writing to the above address. Cash Value 1/100 of 1¢. 9009

20¢

87968

MANUFACTURER COUPON | NO EXPIRATION DATE

87981

SAVE 20¢

when you buy Duncan Hines Angel Food (or three any other Duncan Hines Cake Mixes)

PROCTER & GAMBLE

CONSUMER: Redeem ONLY by purchasing the brand size(s) indicated. May not be reproduced. Void if transferred to any person, firm or group prior to store redemption. You pay any sales tax. Any other use constitutes fraud. **LIMIT ONE COUPON PER PURCHASE.**
DEALER: Sending coupons to **Procter & Gamble,** 2150 Sunnybrook Drive, Cincinnati, Ohio 45237 signifies compliance with "Requirements for Proper Coupon Redemption." Copy available by writing to the above address. Cash Value 1/100 of 1¢. 9009

20¢

87981

5 37000 33120 4